The Skunk
and His Junk

Pam Scheunemann

Consulting Editor, Diane Craig, M.A./Reading Specialist

Published by ABDO Publishing Company, 4940 Viking Drive, Edina, Minnesota 55435.

Printed in the United States.

Credits
Edited by: Pam Price
Curriculum Coordinator: Nancy Tuminelly
Cover and Interior Design and Production: Mighty Media
Photo Credits: AbleStock, Photodisc

Library of Congress Cataloging-in-Publication Data

Scheunemann, Pam, 1955-
    The skunk and his junk / Pam Scheunemann.
        p. cm. -- (First rhymes)
    Includes index.
    ISBN 1-59679-525-5 (hardcover)
    ISBN 1-59679-526-3 (paperback)
        1. English language--Rhyme--Juvenile literature. I. Title. II. Series.

PE1517.S455 2005
808.1--dc22

                                                                          2005048042

SandCastle™ books are created by a professional team of educators, reading specialists, and content developers around five essential components that include phonemic awareness, phonics, vocabulary, text comprehension, and fluency. All books are written, reviewed, and leveled for guided reading and early intervention reading, and designed for use in shared, guided, and independent reading and writing activities to support a balanced approach to literacy instruction.

Let Us Know

After reading the book, SandCastle would like you to tell us your stories about reading. What is your favorite page? Was there something hard that you needed help with? Share the ups and downs of learning to read. We want to hear from you! To get posted on the ABDO Publishing Company Web site, send us e-mail at:

sandcastle@abdopub.com

SandCastle Level: Beginning

-unk

bunk

junk

skunk

sunk

trunk

Here is a 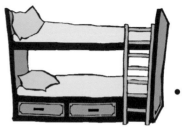 .

This is  .

This is a  .

The ship has 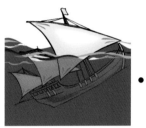 .

Here is a  .

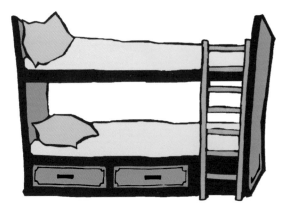

A bunk has two beds.

The junk is old.

A skunk has a
bad smell.

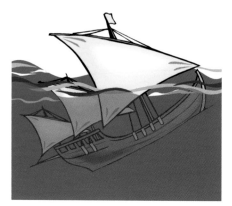

The ship has
sunk in the lake.

You can store
things in a trunk.

The Skunk and His Junk

On a little boat
lived a skunk.

The skunk
slept on a bunk.

The skunk
had lots of junk
in his bunk.

The skunk
took the junk
from his bunk
and put it in a trunk.

The skunk bumped the trunk with the junk from his bunk.

The trunk went kerplunk.

"Oh, no!" said the skunk. "My junk has sunk!"

About SandCastle™

A professional team of educators, reading specialists, and content developers created the SandCastle™ series to support young readers as they develop reading skills and strategies and increase their general knowledge. The SandCastle™ series has four levels that correspond to early literacy development in young children. The levels are provided to help teachers and parents select the appropriate books for young readers.

Emerging Readers
(no flags)

Beginning Readers
(1 flag)

Transitional Readers
(2 flags)

Fluent Readers
(3 flags)

These levels are meant only as a guide. All levels are subject to change.

To see a complete list of SandCastle™ books and other nonfiction titles from ABDO Publishing Company, visit **www.abdopub.com** or contact us at:
4940 Viking Drive, Edina, Minnesota 55435 • 1-800-800-1312 • fax: 1-952-831-1632